COME ON IN!

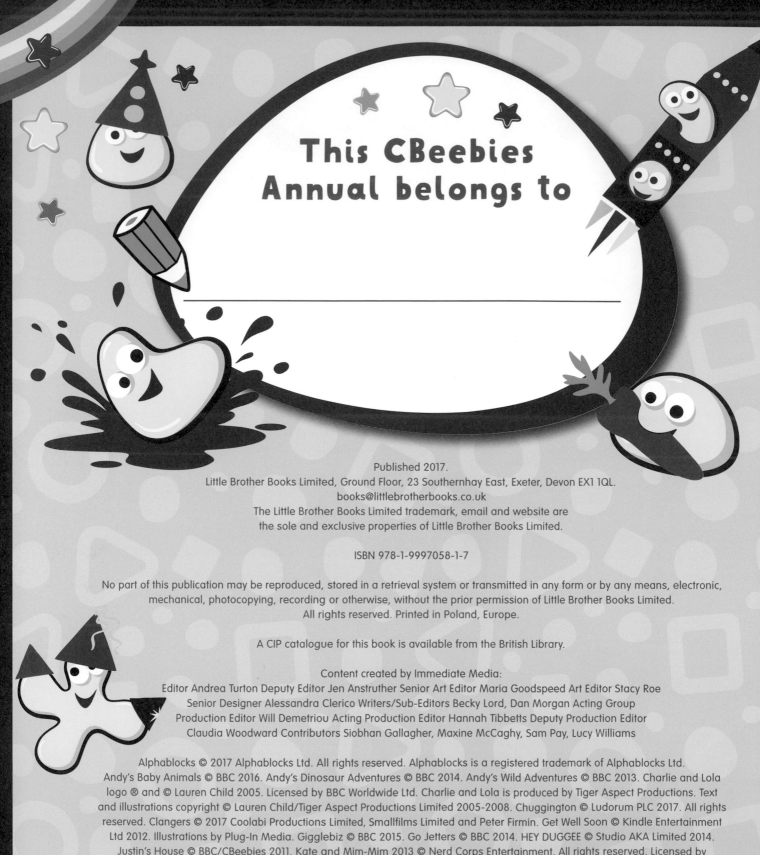

This CBeebies Annual belongs to

_____

Published 2017.
Little Brother Books Limited, Ground Floor, 23 Southernhay East, Exeter, Devon EX1 1QL.
books@littlebrotherbooks.co.uk
The Little Brother Books Limited trademark, email and website are
the sole and exclusive properties of Little Brother Books Limited.

ISBN 978-1-9997058-1-7

A CIP catalogue for this book is available from the British Library.

Content created by Immediate Media:
Editor Andrea Turton Deputy Editor Jen Anstruther Senior Art Editor Maria Goodspeed Art Editor Stacy Roe
Senior Designer Alessandra Clerico Writers/Sub-Editors Becky Lord, Dan Morgan Acting Group
Production Editor Will Demetriou Acting Production Editor Hannah Tibbetts Deputy Production Editor
Claudia Woodward Contributors Siobhan Gallagher, Maxine McCaghy, Sam Pay, Lucy Williams

LB BOOKS

BBC

Who's inside?

5

All about ME!

Say hello to your CBeebies House friends and tell them all about YOU!

My **name** is:

Write and **say** hello:

hello

Hi, I'm Andy. It's nice to meet you!

I look like this!

Draw your **face** here.

Hello, Duggee!

He's the fun-loving leader of the Squirrel Club!

Duggee looks after 5 Squirrels. Can you say their names?

Woof!

BETTY   **NORRIE**   **HAPPY**   **ROLY**   **TAG**

Duggee

Join the dots to see Duggee's favourite thing!

Woooof!

HEY DUGGEE

Duggee loves collecting leaves.
Draw lines to sort them into pairs.

9

Pirates!

Aharrr, m'hearties! Let's do the Swashbuckle salute with Gem.

Colour a gem each time you do the action!

1 Let me see you marching...

2 Put your hand on your heart...

3 Eye patch!

4 Pirate hat!

5 Swashbuckle cheer, aharrr!

Just imagine...

Guide Monty and Jimmy Jones through the fish to their imaginary tropical island.

Monty Kazoop is a boy with a big imagination.

WOW! Look at these colourful fish.

Jimmy Jones is Monty's pet pig!

How many of these fish can you see?

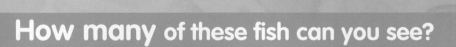

12

Welcome to the island!

13

Be happy, be healthy!

It's important to look after your body by eating healthily.

Food wheel

- Vegetables
- Fruit
- Meat, fish and eggs
- Milk and cheese
- Bread, cereals and pasta

Eat something from each section of the food wheel every day for a healthy, balanced diet!

14

Niagara Falls

1 ON JET PAD...

One morning, the Go Jetters were in trouble! **"Jet Pad power is at 10%!"** said Lars. "What are we going to do?"

We need more power right now!

But how can Jet Pad get power from a waterfall?

Wait and see!

2

"Don't worry, we're in North America and heading for one of the **biggest waterfalls** in the world," said Ubercorn. **"But the Jet Pad needs electricity, not water!"** said Xuli. "Hold on to your hoods, Lars and Xuli, all will be revealed," chuckled Ubercorn.

3 ON GRIM HQ

Meanwhile, the Grimbots were busy spraying mud all over Grim HQ. **"Very nice, Grimbots. It looks so grim and grimy,"** said Grandmaster Glitch. **"But we need even more mud. Quick, I see a clean spot!"**

I love MUD!

4 Just then, Jet Pad zoomed past Grim HQ. As it whooshed by, it caught one of the Grimbot's mud tubes and **dragged Grim HQ along behind it.** Grim HQ splashed through a river and all the mud washed off!

Whoosh!

BEEP!

Welcome to Niagara Falls!

5 Soon, the Go Jetters arrived at their destination. **"Go wild for... Niagara Falls,"** sang Ubercorn. "Wow! That's bigger than big," said Lars. "Oh no," said Foz. "Jet Pad power is at 2%. And 2% plus bigger than big waterfall equals huge splash landing... **I can't look."**

6 "We really need electricity!" said Xuli. "Relax, Go Jetters. **All this powerful water makes electricity,"** replied Ubercorn. "The Niagara River flows into a power station and turns a generator, **which makes electricity."**

7 Ubercorn hooked Jet Pad up to the Niagara Falls power station. It started to charge, then, all of a sudden, **the electricity stopped.** "The power station's not working and, look, the water's turned to mud!" cried Lars. "But why?" wondered Kyan. "There's only one way to find out... **to the Vroomster,**" said Xuli.

8 The Go Jetters whizzed along in the Vroomster until... **"Look. It's Grandmaster Glitch!** He's sucking up mud from the riverbed with a giant straw to make Grim HQ all dirty. That's why the water has turned to mud," said Kyan. "Time to fix this mess," cried Xuli.

GLITCHED!

9 Xuli flew the Vroomster right down to Grim HQ. "Xuli, can you hold the Vroomster here?" asked Kyan. "Not for long," said Xuli. "What's the plan?" **"Click-Ons!" cried Kyan.**

Bah! Those No Jetters aren't going to ruin my fun.

10 Ubercorn gave Kyan the G.O. Grab Click-On. It was time for him to do some **fantastic gymnastics!** He swooshed down from the Vroomster and squeezed Glitch's mud-sucking straw with the G.O. Grab. **Water rushed in and washed all the mud away.**

You did it, Go Jetters!

11 The Go Jetters had fixed the glitch. The water was flowing and the power station was working again. "Jet Pad power is at 100%! Great work, Go Jetters," cheered Ubercorn. **"Geographic!" cried Lars.**

Oh, grimbles!

THE END

Wordplay

Write, search and tick to finish
these Alphablocks puzzles.

Fill in the words using the pictures to help.
All the words contain the letter n.

tin

n

net

bun

bin

Terrific!
Can you spot a
word that begins
with t?

t

C

Tick each word as you find it in the wordsearch. Look across and down!

x	b	e	e
c	a	p	z
d	g	o	k
e	p	d	n

I wonder where the words are?

W

bag

cap

pod

bee

23

Rainbow!

Finish the rainbow with your crayons.

Copy Justin to learn the signs for the colours.

 **red**

 **orange**

 **yellow**

 **green**

 **blue**

rainbow

colour

25

Pond Princess

Read this story about when Sarah and Duck went for a royal walk around the pond!

When you see these pictures in the story, say the names.  **Sarah**  **Duck**  **Rainbow**

It was a lovely sunny day, and  and  were at the park, sitting on

their bench. threw some bread to the ducks in the pond. **"Quack,"**

said the ducks. They were all looking at . They wanted to give her a

crown. It seemed that she was their princess! **"Pond Princess?"**

asked . "Quack, quack," quacked the ducks, nodding their heads.

 was very excited that was a pond princess. "Quack" he said,

happily. So put on her crown. She thought she should give

a special name. So she made into **of the bread slice.**

Next,  and her ducks went for a **royal walk.**

It started to rain, and the ducks all stared at . But then the **sun** came

out and an **old friend** appeared. "!" said . "Hello!" said .

"You're Pond Princess! I'd know that crown anywhere." The ducks stared

at . "I don't know what they want me to do," whispered . But

knew. "The pond princess has only one job... to choose a **king** or

queen of the pond," said . ", I make you king of the pond!"

said . And happily shone his bright colours on the ducks.

What a royal day!

The
end

Ocean

The Octonauts are looking for colourful sea creatures. Make the page nice and bright for them!

Shiver me whiskers!

28

explorers

Topsy and Tim!

Let's find out all about the terrific twins.

I like to whizz about on my scooter!

Write her name.

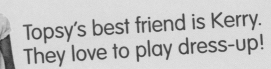

Topsy

Topsy's best friend is Kerry. They love to play dress-up!

Draw me dressed as an astronaut!

Write his name.

Tim

I love riding my bike to the park with Topsy!

Topsy and Tim

He is 5

Draw a picture of you with your best friend here.

Tim's best friend is Tony Welch. They have lots of fun together!

Fishy picture

Grab your pencils and give these fish some colourful patterns.

I've had a swimmingly good idea!

Now draw your own fish in a bowl...

Draw around
your hand.

Colour it in and
add an eye.

I'm going
to call him
Jaws!

33

Find the Froglets

The Froglets are hiding.
Help the Clangers find them!

Trace over the numbers when you find the Froglets.

  green Froglet

  purple Froglets

orange Froglets

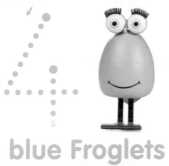

blue Froglets

yellow Froglets

The fun run

Can Raymond stop worrying about being slow and just have some fun? Read this story to find out!

1 "You're too fast for me."

One day, the Veggies were playing tag. Poor Raymond was very slow. He couldn't catch anyone.

2 "I'm just a slow squash."

"I'm so slow," he told Mr. Bloom sadly. "You don't have to be fast," said Mr. Bloom.

3 He told Raymond that running should be fun. "Why don't we have a fun run?" he smiled.

4

The Veggies loved the idea. Especially when they found out they could do it in fancy dress!

5

Off I go!

WHOOSH!

"5-4-3-2-1, GO!" said Mr. Bloom.
Colin the runner bean raced off.

6

Mr. Bloom's
right!

"Remember, it's a fun run, so
have FUN!" said Mr. Bloom.

7

BOING!

Raymond ran off but he tripped
and fell onto the trampoline...

8

Almost
at the finish,
Raymond.

BOING! He landed in the
sandpit... right next to Colin!

9

HOORAY!

And guess what? They crossed
the finish line TOGETHER!

10

Hooray!

Raymond felt very proud.
"We did it!" he cheered.

The end (37)

Training time

Wilson

Wilson loves going on adventures and learning new things.

Brewster

Brewster likes to help his friends.

Koko

CHUGGINGTON

Koko is always ready to race!

Draw around the shapes to finish the signs.

Illustrated by Emma Holt.

Tiger

Find out all about this amazing big cat!

Trace the dotty letters.

ROAR

Every tiger has its own pattern of stripes. When the tiger goes hunting, the stripes help it to hide in the grass or behind trees.

Patterns or colours that help animals hide are called camouflage.

A tiger's roar can be heard for miles!

Colour the tiger's stripes black.

Playing is good for baby animals! It helps them to grow strong.

Kittens

Find out how these baby cats love to explore and play!

Amazing BABY Animals

Kittens have a good sense of smell. They use their noses to explore the world.

Kittens pounce and chase other kittens as well as their mums. It's their way of playing!

Which one is a kitten's nose? Circle the answer.

Which trail leads this kitten to its playmates?

a   b   c

43

Let's move!

There's a lot going on in the playground!
Trace the trails and the words to join the fun.

Start!

Kid is

hopping

on his way to see Finlay.

Timmy is

running

in a race.

Finish!

HOP! HOP! HOP! HOP!

Mittens is

walking

on her way to see the flowers.

Toy spider

Woolly is Tig's cuddly toy spider.
They have lots of fun together!

Write the numbers to
count Woolly's legs.

Woolly has ___ legs.

Woolly always knows how Tig feels.
Draw a line from each picture to the
word that matches Tig's mood.

scared

grumpy

happy

puzzled

surprised

How do you feel today? Draw your face:

Colour me happy!

Kate has gone to Mimiloo to see her friends!
Finish the picture with lots of bright colours.

Here's a picture to help you.

Mim

Gobble

Tack

Mim

Kate

Lily

Boomer

51

Grimbots!

6 Grimbots have been glitched.
Can you spot them in the big picture?

Tick the boxes
when you find these
glitched Grimbots!

52

Dodge's dogs

Let's find out about Dodge's furry friends!

Dogs come in all shapes and sizes!

Dogs have fur which needs to be brushed to keep them clean and healthy.

Trace the dotty lines, then colour the brush.

Dogs need lots of space to run around. Big dogs need to be taken for walks twice a day!

Race your fingers along the paw prints from 1 to 10.

All dogs need to be fed a healthy diet. It's important to make sure they have fresh food and water every day.

Just like you, dogs need healthy food!

Follow the steps to draw a cute puppy.

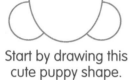

Start by drawing this cute puppy shape.

Then add some puppy paws...

...and finally add a puppy face and tail!

I really like your picture!

Silly spotting

Wave hello to Justin and his friends.
Then spot 6 differences in the pictures.

Write a number when you find each difference.

1 2 3 4 5 6

Justin Robert Little
Monster Cat

Colour the letters, then say the name.

Justin

Count on us!

Circle the correct Numberblocks
to finish the sums.

Colour this number line,
then use it to help you count.

1 2 3 4 5

2 + 2 =

4

2

2 + 3 =

3

4

5

What's growing?

60

Join the dots to see what Duggee and the Squirrels have grown, then colour the picture.

5 •   • 6
4 •
3 •
2 •
1 •   • 10

• 7
• 8
• 9

5 •   • 6
4 •   • 7
3 •   • 8
2 •   • 9
1 •   • 10

3 •   4 •   5 •   6 •   7 •
2 •
• 8
1 •   • 9
10

5 •   6 •   7 •   • 8
4 •   • 9
3 •   • 10
2 •   • 11
1 •   • 12

61

Illustrated by Ian Cunliffe.

Letter match

Trace the dotty letters, then draw lines to all the words that start with the same letter.

C is for carrot.

The letter b is for book.

butterfly

book

cabbage

carrot

S is for strawberry.

An acorn begins with a.

Peter Rabbit

acorn

snail

strawberry

apple

Slops and ladders game!

Finish

30 Do the **Swashbuckle salute!**	**29**	**28**	
16 Pretend to **flap** your wings **3 times** like Squawk!	**17** Colour me in!	**18**	**19**
15	**14**	**13**	**12**
Start	**1**	**2** Run on the spot like a busy pirate for **10 seconds.**	**3**

You did it!

It is the biggest snake in the world!

Follow the dotty line along the snake.

OCTONAUTS

Mmm, tassssty!

Time for a sssnake sssnack, matey!

First, ask your grown-up to cut a bagel in half and then arrange it into a snake shape.

Spread on cream cheese.

Use an olive for the eye.

Use veggies to make patterns.

Cucumber peel makes a good tongue!

Tee hee hee!

Have a giggle at these jokes and colour in the funny pictures.

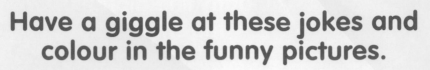

Hello, Gigglers! Can you tell me a joke?

What do you call a smelly fairy?

What do crocodiles like to play?

Stinkerbell!

SNAP!

Why are babies good at football? Because they're always dribbling!

What do you call a dancing lamb? A baa-llerina!

What do snowmen have for breakfast? Snowflakes!

Why do cows have bells?

What time is it when an elephant sits on your fence?

Because their horns don't work!

Time to get a new fence!

Eggboxosaurus

Get creative and make a dinosaur out of recycled egg boxes.

Tick off the items when you have them.

 2 clean egg boxes

 safe scissors and glue

 red & yellow tissue paper

 paints and brushes

Your dino could look like this!

Do a big roar like this dino!

ROAR!

1
Paint an egg box and add some spots.

Ask a grown-up to help with the cutting.

2
Cut out 4 egg holders from the other egg box. **Paint** some feet, then **stick** them on the painted egg box.

glue

3
Draw a face on another egg holder. **Join** it to the egg box using a thick, rolled-up piece of tissue paper.

4
Do the same for the tail. **Stick** a big ball of tissue paper at the end to make a fierce club tail!

5
Finish your Eggboxosaurus with twisted tissue paper spikes!

Great job!

Illustrated by Sonia Canals.

71

Fruity faces

Get scribbling to put some funny faces on these fruits for Charlie and Lola.

Mr Apple looks happy, Lola!

Jack and the

Settle down for this magical story...

Once upon a time,
there was a little boy called Jack.

Jack and his mummy were so poor that they were forced to sell their cow at the market to buy food.

On his way to the market, Jack met a lady who gave him **5 magic beans** for the cow.

But when he got home, his mummy was very cross and she threw the beans out of the window!

The next day Jack looked out of the window – the beans had grown into a

giant beanstalk that reached high into the sky! Jack climbed up the beanstalk and at the top he saw a huge castle.

Jack felt the ground shake: **"Fee, fi, fo, fum. Watch out, everyone – here I come!"** A great, big, greedy giant appeared, holding a hen that laid golden eggs.

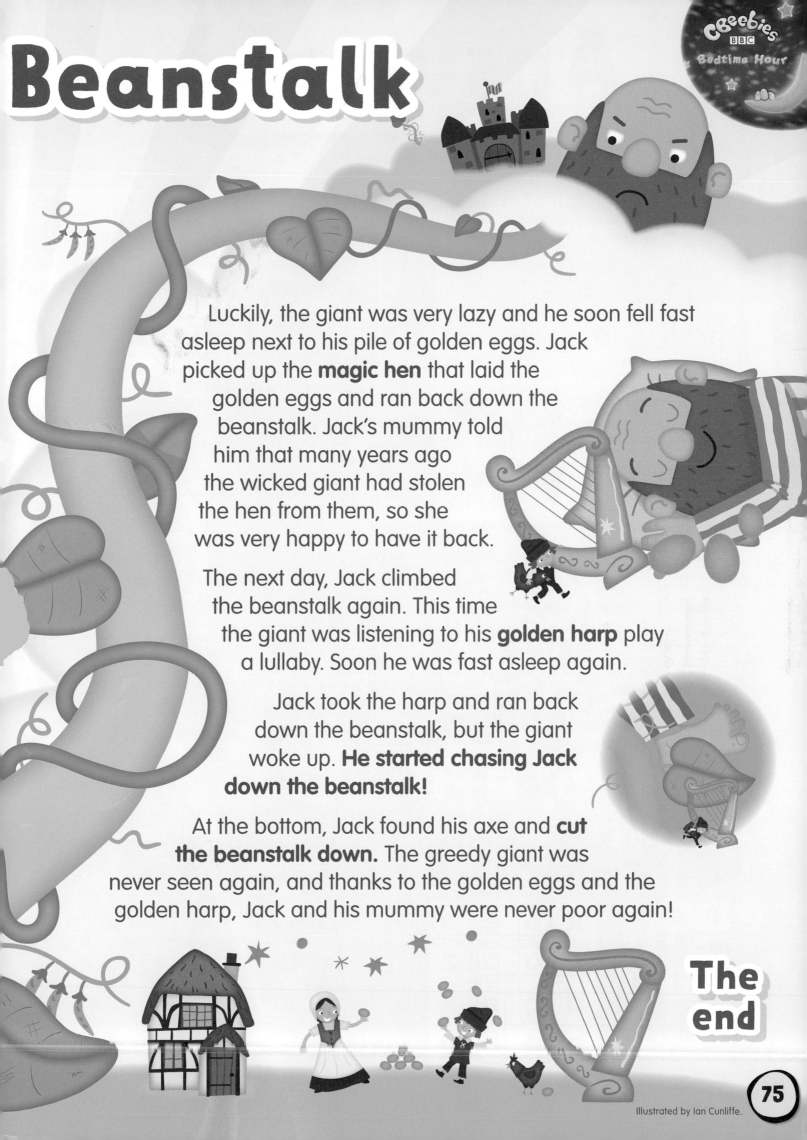

Beanstalk

Luckily, the giant was very lazy and he soon fell fast asleep next to his pile of golden eggs. Jack picked up the **magic hen** that laid the golden eggs and ran back down the beanstalk. Jack's mummy told him that many years ago the wicked giant had stolen the hen from them, so she was very happy to have it back.

The next day, Jack climbed the beanstalk again. This time the giant was listening to his **golden harp** play a lullaby. Soon he was fast asleep again.

Jack took the harp and ran back down the beanstalk, but the giant woke up. **He started chasing Jack down the beanstalk!**

At the bottom, Jack found his axe and **cut the beanstalk down.** The greedy giant was never seen again, and thanks to the golden eggs and the golden harp, Jack and his mummy were never poor again!

The end

Illustrated by Ian Cunliffe.

Answers

Pages 8-9

Duggee's favourite thing is a bone!

Pages 12-13

 6 3 4 2 5

Pages 22-23

net
bun
bin

x	b	e	e
c	a	p	z
d	g	o	k
e	p	d	n

Pages 34-35

Page 43

The kitten's nose looks like this.

Trail b leads the kitten to its playmates.

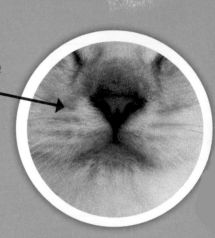

Pages 46-47

scared

grumpy

happy

puzzled

surprised

Pages 48-49

There are

6

radishes.

Pages 52-53

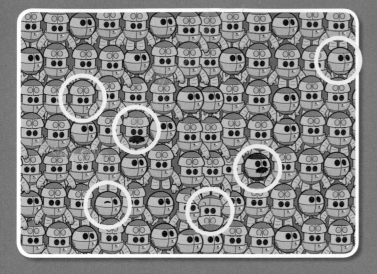

Pages 56-57

Pages 58-59

 +  =  　  +  =

Pages 62-63

a words 　 **a**corn 　 **a**pple

b words 　 **b**utterfly 　 **b**ook

c words 　 **c**abbage 　 **c**arrot

s words 　 **s**trawberry 　 **s**nail

Pages 66-67

This is the Amazon jungle. →

The pattern on the anaconda is **stripy.**